How to Make Money wit

Best Selling Wooden Crafts an

Entrepreneur Series

Mendon Cottage Books

JD-Biz Publishing

Download Free Books!

http://MendonCottageBooks.com

Our books are available at

1. Amazon.com
2. Barnes and Noble
3. Itunes
4. Kobo
5. Smashwords
6. Google Play Books

Download Free Books!

http://MendonCottageBooks.com

Table of Contents

Introduction 7

Wood Lathe 7

Important Decisions to Make Before Starting Your Sales: 11

Pricing is Critical for Successful Sales: 12

Making Money for a Living or Just Making Some Extra Cash: 13

    1. Unique and innovative products sell! 13

    2. Craft shows are a good opportunity for sellers: 14

    3. Make money through teaching your skill to others: 15

    4. Online portals are fast and easy ways to sell your creations: 15

    5. Get connected with retailers and store operators: 16

Prepare Your Workshop for Your Business Venture: 18

    1. Preparation: 18

    2. Sweep up around your lathe: 18

    3. Clean and organize your turning and other tools 19

    4. Organize your wood and off cuts: 20

    5. Examining your tools: 21

    6. Preparing your workshop for safety: 21

Wood Turning for the Two Essential P's: Passion and Profit 23

    The transformation from a hobbyist into a professional wood turner or worker: 23

Make money after retirement: 24

Some recommendations for turners working for profit: 24

Bestselling Woodturning Projects 29

Product selection is critical: 29

Product demand is essential for success: 29

Take ideas from various sources: 29

Factors underlying the product selection: 30

Current Categories of Wood Turning Projects: 33

Bestselling Wood Turning Products in the Market: 35

Simple wooden bowls: 35

A dried fruit dish: 36

Wooden candle holders: 37

Handles or knobs for kitchen utensils: 37

Serving trays: 38

Clocks: 39

Decorative items for any room: 39

Wooden office utilities: 40

Wooden rolling pins: 40

Chop sticks, spoons and servers: 42

Pens: 42

Best Selling Wood Crafts to Make and Sell 46

Woodcraft is ancient: 46

Making wooden objects for profit: 47

Some Product Categories to Work On: 49

Children's toys: 49

Baby cradles and cribs: 51

Bookcases: 52

Picture frames: 52

Boxes: 53

Birdhouses: 54

Blanket chests: 55

Wooden spoons and ladles: 56

Name plates and planters: 57

Small wooden tables: 57

Wooden stools: 57

Wine stands and racks: 59

Wooden arm chairs: 59

Paper weights: 60

Wooden tablet stands: 60

Drawer organizers: 61

Office trays: 62

Wall shelves and racks: 62

Wooden pots and planters: 62

Final Thoughts about Transforming Your Wood Crafting Ideas and Turning a Hobby into a Money-Making Activity: 64

1.   Attitude is everything: 65

2.   Quality is everything: 66

3.   Be optimistic: 67

4.   It won't happen overnight: 67

5.   Maintain good supplier relations: 68

6.   Pricing is critical: 68

Best of Luck! 69

Publisher 80

Introduction

Are you a hobbyist who likes to work with wood? Is using a wood lathe your skill polishing platform? Have you ever thought of making money using this craft? Selling your wood lathe projects for profitable margins can be a very lucrative business for amateurs. This is not the only craft or hobby that can be converted into a profession or a means for earning a living. There are many more as well. Below you will find a detailed view of how and why a wood lathe can help you make money, and at the same time remain an interesting and wonderful hobby for all the wood craft lovers.

For those of you who are reading about this for the first time, here is a brief description of a wood lathe, and all you need to know about wood lathing projects:

Wood Lathe

A lathe is an essential piece of equipment used in many arts and crafts. It consists of a rotating center platform that is attached to an axis. It can be used for the creation of items that are symmetrical in shape from the point of rotation of the lathe. You can cut, sand, knurl, drill, deform, turn and do a number of different artistic functions with this piece of equipment.

The lathe is utilized in various industries and crafts, such as:

- Wood turning
- Metal works
- Metal spinning projects
- Thermal spray processes
- Reclamation of objects
- Glass work projects
- Pottery making and sculpturing

The most commonly used lathe is the wood lathe. It has been employed in the wood turning business for many years. It is different from other forms of woodworking because in this process the object keeps on moving while the tools are used in a stationery position on the rotating object. Different types of cuts and shapes are given to the piece of wood placed on the wood lathe to turn it into a functional piece of art. The designing and intricacy of shape given to the product reflects the expertise of the wood turner and his craftsmanship qualities.

Although the wood lathe is one of most primitive forms of manual machines used by mankind, it has been combined with the latest technology through the employment of the CNC lathe or turners. This involves the use of a pointed tool utilized for creating cuts on a piece of wood rotating on the lathe. The CNC turning is done by placing the tool just parallel to the rotating surface.

The wood lathe can be used for a variety of designs depending on the blades used in the cutting process. Various widths, shapes, and angles of blades are used to create different shapes and designs with the wooden material placed in the center. Wide blades are mostly used for bigger shapes while pointed blades are used for more detail designs and cuts.

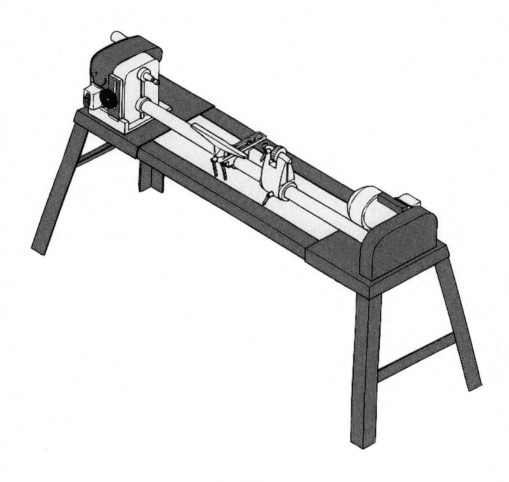

Wood lathes are used in combination with other smaller manual tools as well. Sandpaper is one of the essential tools used for shaping and smoothing the wooden objects. Instead of holding the wooden block by hand, the object is fixed on the lathe in the center and then spun. The sand paper is held next to it helping in the shaping process. The use of a wood lathe in the process makes it easier and less time consuming for the craftsman.

The various types of products commercially created using a wood lathe include things like:

- Decorative items
- Spindles
- Wooden bowls
- Baseball bats
- Pens
- And other cylindrical and circular objects.

Important Decisions to Make Before Starting Your Sales:

If you consider selling the wood lathe projects that you have created, you must keep in mind a number of underlying factors as well. These factors may include things like:

- What exactly are you offering for sale?
- What price will you ask for each product?
- Have you incorporated all factors in the price?
- Factors like labor, raw materials, facility expenses, equipment and tools are vital
- The cost of the kits, glues, sandpapers, finishing items, wax and polishing materials need to be incorporated into the price
- Are you selling your wood lathe projects as a means to supplement your existing earnings or is it an exclusive means of earning your living?

These are a few preliminary questions that you need to answer before you actually go ahead with your wood turning business venture.

Pricing is Critical for Successful Sales:

When starting such a business, most people find it difficult to come up with the right price for their products. They do not want to price them too cheaply nor do they want to charge too high end prices. The latter would definitely scare the customers away even before they make the purchase while the former might undermine the quality and craftsmanship of the product. Selling it for too low a price can also irritate other wood turners in the market. While you may in this type of work for the love of it, but even then, you need to follow the rules and ethics of the business markets.

You not only need to consider the cost of raw materials used in making the product as there are many other things to consider. Think about all the effort and time that you have spent in making the piece.

For a hobbyist who likes to spend time in his or her wood workshop, working on projects and creating masterpieces, and then earning some money from those pieces can be a great advantage. There are many who would rather give away their creations as gifts and souvenirs to others, but this doesn't usually go on endlessly. Earning some extra money has never hurt anyone. And if you are able to convert your passion and love for wood turning into your profession, nothing could be more satisfying and fulfilling than this.

Making Money for a Living or Just Making Some Extra Cash:

The foremost thing that you need to understand before opting for a wood lathe profit making business is to ask yourself whether you want to make money or make a living. Being a skill driven industry, there is a lot of competition in this market. Those who are earning their living with this craft have long years of experience and expertise. They have a good reputation in the market with a large number of satisfied customers willing to spread the word around.

Either way, you need to maintain the intensity of your passion and strengthen your faith in your skills. Realization and reiteration of your creating and selling abilities will help you compete with greater motivation and endurance. Try to reach the standards prevalent in the market and match your creativity and product quality with the products of the best players in the wood turning market. Keep your pricing competitive and attractive for the first-time customers.

1. Unique and innovative products sell!

Be innovative and creative about the products you want to sell in the market. Your products should stand out among the competition. Uniqueness of offering can definitely help you gain advantage over your competitor. The most commonly available products in the wood lathe market these days are pens and kitchen items. Salad bowls and dried fruit trays are very popular items. But you don't need to restrict your offerings to specific product categories but remain artistic with a number of decorative artifacts and unique new items.

2. Craft shows are a good opportunity for sellers:

Taking part in craft shows and artistic gallery exhibitions is a good way to display your products in the existing markets. For the more professional workers, this is a great platform to show their creative and artistic sides. You can exhibit your creations with great craftsmanship and skills. Those who like and appreciate your work will be willing to pay any price for them. The craft shows help you to start selling your products and to expand to a greater market, as well as reach larger potential markets.

3. Make money through teaching your skill to others:

Giving crafting and wood turning lessons is another very popular way of making money with your skills. Expansion of your income or earnings can increase if you transfer your skills to others in an effective manner. Many woodworking lovers and turner enthusiasts are willing to spend large amounts on wood lathe lessons and classes. Starting with beginners, you can vary the prices and features of each lesson according to the level of advancement in technique and skills. All you need is to be able to give clear instructions and some reading material for your students. For first timers, try to teach a few friends in the beginning and get their feedback regarding your lessons. Make improvements where necessary to make your classes more productive.

4. Online portals are fast and easy ways to sell your creations:

Online or internet markets are some of the most lucrative business industries these days. With everything available at online stores, the people's need to physically go out and buy stuff is diminishing with time. Selling your wood lathe projects on the internet is a good option. Starting with single items, you can create customized products specific to the orders placed by customers.

Putting your products up for sale on various selling websites like Etsy, Craigslist, and eBay is a good way to promote your products. With more people seeing your product, the chances of sales will also increase. Although these websites may charge a commission on the sales, the profits will be generated from the large amount of sales. You could also opt for starting and managing your own selling website or portal. Technology has become easy and simple. You can initiate a blog that not only offers your products for sale but which also provides good information about the wood lathe crafts to other enthusiasts. Highlighting your products with pictures and even videos is much more convenient and cheaper through this medium.

Although this is a good option, there are still many people who find it difficult to make a buying decision on the internet. They strongly feel the need to touch and fondle the piece of wood before making the decision to buy it.

5. Get connected with retailers and store operators:

Find out if there are businesses in your area that can display and sell your products in their stores or outlets. Get some space or a shelf from them and promote your products in their commercial outlets. You could also get a booth or stall at local flea markets, funfairs, and carnivals.

Once you have decided that you are going to make money from your wood lathing projects, you need to prepare yourself as a businessman starting a new venture. Making products and objects that you love and then selling them to someone else could be the venture we all dream about or what motivational speakers often talk about.

Prepare Your Workshop for Your Business Venture:

Apart from all the creativity and passion, you also need to prepare your workshop and turn it into the production hub for creating and selling your master pieces. Below are six important tips that you must remember before starting your wood lathe business venture:

1. Preparation:

You need to have a large number of cardboard boxes and containers. These will be utilized for holding various types of small raw materials, such as screws, nails, glues, etc. Having glass jars or containers with clear walls is also a good idea to keep everything visible and easy to access. Labeling the containers with labels or a marker can also make things more convenient.

You also need some storage space and shelves in your workshop. This is the place that stores all the necessary items and which you can reach out to while the wood turning is in process. Covering the shelves with transparent plastic sheets or other material, such as an old sheet, can help save them from dust and dirt accumulation.

2. Sweep up around your lathe:

Keep your wood lathe clean and tidy. Make sure your workshop and all the related tools have been cleared of all the leftover debris and sawdust. Having a good sweeping broom and brush is a must in a wood lathe workshop.

Some of artists are too lazy to clean up after they have finished a project. But if you plan to use your workshop as a display center as well, you need to make it attractive for potential customers. This does not mean that you need to keep it spotlessly clean, but a little sweep here and there is advisable. Keep a large garbage bin in an easy to reach place to throw away all the shavings and debris. You should also line them with garbage bags to ensure easy removal. Using gloves and a face mask while sweeping the shavings is always a good idea to protect yourself from any unnecessary health problems.

3. Clean and organize your turning and other tools

Place all your equipment and tools in one place that can be assessed in an easy manner. Clean your tools properly and sharpen them if necessary. The waxing and oiling of tool handles is also needed from time to time to enhance their lifespan. Check the tools for safety before starting on a project. If you have some tools missing, replace them for future projects. If any of the tools have undergone irreparable wear and tear, they should also be replaced.

How you organize your tools can help you save a lot of time and allow you to carry on your work without any interruptions. If you are a carpenter who utilizes electronic equipment for cutting or polishing, it is essential to keep their batteries charged and functional at all times. Keeping spare batteries in the workshop is also a good idea.

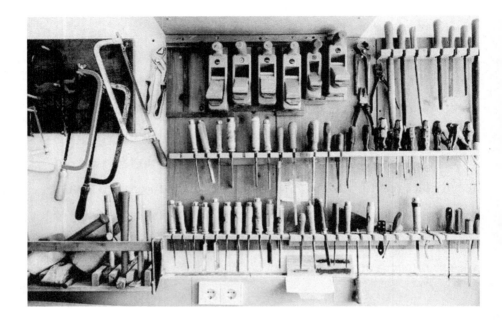

4. Organize your wood and off cuts:

The basic raw material for every project using a wood lathe is obviously wood. Along with larger pieces, you also need to maintain storage for smaller pieces of various sizes and lengths. Keep them stored in cardboard boxes and mark them with a pen and paper. Always do a random sorting of all the leftover pieces after you have finished a project. A missing wood piece can slow down or halt an entire project until you find the right piece. So, for saving time, effort and money, do not throw away your leftover pieces. You can also mark the boxes according to the type of wood that you are using in your projects.

5. Examining your tools:

If you utilize power tools and electronic equipment, ensure their maintenance over a specific time period. Check their power cables and accessibility to the wood lathe. Keep their blades sharpened and oil all their necessary parts for smooth working. From time to time check their surfaces for accumulated rust.

6. Preparing your workshop for safety:

With any type of lathing project, safety and protective gear is a must. In order to avoid any unfortunate accidents while using sharp blades and cutters, always give priority to safety. Always assess the safety and protection measures of your work shop to remain proactive in the business.

- Buying a first aid box with all the necessary requirements and medications is a must. Replenish the used items every month to avoid using up any of the necessary items. You must keep a fire extinguishing equipment in the shop as wood items are highly flammable.

- You should keep dust masks and gloves in a handy place in the workshop. Protective transparent glasses are also a must for even the smallest projects.
- Floors and surfaces of the workshop should be clear and leveled. The chances of tripping and slipping should be minimized to avoid injuries.
- Your workplace should have proper lighting with bright and comfortable visibility.
- The lathe and storage of wood blocks should be firm and secure. You do not want things to fall off while you are working on them.

These few steps will help ensure the readiness of your workshop. They are advantageous in every way. Whether you are doing it as a hobby or as a professional wood turner, these tips will be very useful for your safety and comfort while working in the wood lathe workshop.

Wood Turning for the Two Essential P's: Passion and Profit

The transformation from a hobbyist into a professional wood turner or worker:

Once you have prepared yourself and your workshop for a wood lathe profit-making venture, you need to understand the ways of making money through this project. Whether you are a new comer or an expert in the field, making money out of your skill is the best thing you can do.

In general, there are three categories of wood turners in the market. They are:

- Full-time woodworkers
- Part-time woodworkers
- Hobbyists

The first category consists of people who earn all their income from this work while the second category of workers earn smaller amounts. The hobbyists are those who do not earn from their work. They cherish their skills and crafts as an enjoyable hobby only.

Make money after retirement:

Turning a hobby into a profession does not mean that you have to be very young to make money. Many people adopt different crafts after they have retired from their existing professions and jobs. It's like finding an alternative earning option after your actual lifetime career. So why not bring in some money while you actually enjoy yourself in the workshop.

Most people who work with a wood lathe start by making small objects for their own use. Then they move on to things that can be gifted and presented to others. The more advanced category of workers start producing artistic projects that show their creative instincts. As you continue to pursue this hobby over a longer period of time, the number objects stored in your workshop or garage will start to grow. Most of the time, you won't know what to do with them. So, it's a good idea to start selling them for money. If you are hobbyist, you can spend that money on tools and new workshop supplies. It will help in managing the costs of your favorite hobby while you spend time doing what you enjoy. But if you want to earn a living from this, then you will need to move ahead of the financial break-even point.

Some recommendations for turners working for profit:

Next are some important considerations for making money by using a wood lathe:

- **Products**: Before starting the business venture, you need to make a decision about the products you want to make. Like all other designers, you need to select a product line. This is not just a random thought. You must think about the things which people would like to buy. Your products should be able to fulfill a need or a requirement.

- **Market research is compulsory:** Like all other businesses, wood lathing also requires you to carry out some market research. Gathering the necessary information about potential customers and the industry is a necessary step forward. Stock your workshop with the required supplies, planned designs, patterns and woodturning kits of the selected product line. Select some good and reliable suppliers in the market. You also need to create some products as display models and exhibits for future orders.

- **Carry out product tests or market sampling:** Show the samples to potential customers around your area. Ask for improvement suggestions and innovative ideas from family members, friends and coworkers.

- **Product line selection:** Initially you will have to make a product line of at least 5 to 8 items. You can find some good ideas by looking at what is currently happening in the industry. Look at the products of existing wood turners in the market and find out what products are selling. You can also get inspiration from woodcraft catalogs and social media websites and communities. Often the bestselling items are highlighted on the covers of the catalogues, while the not-so-attractive products are found after in the center pages.

- **Attend craft shows for new ideas:** The bestselling products are also given top places in craft shows and exhibitions. Attending the local wood crafting shows and funfairs is a good way to get ideas about your potential product line and the products that you need to offer. You need to be highly attentive and observant in order to identify the products that are in high demand by customers. You can also take ideas from other products that are not created from wood. If they are in big demand, you can convert them into wooden versions as well.

- **Remain updated on latest trends through magazines and websites:** If you are a wood- craft enthusiast, you probably know about a number of magazines and websites that provide information and updates about the current trends in the industry. They often have ideas and articles that highlight the bestselling products made with a wood lathe and how these can be offered to the customers. They also provide information about upcoming trade shows and fairs where you can promote and display your products.

- **Create Prototypes and Samples:** Once you have decided on the list of items that you want to create and sell through your woodworking skills, you need to produce some prototypes and samples. These should be in small quantities that can be displayed and offered for sale in shows or in some stores. Analyze the response that you get from the potential customers. Note down the sales patterns and demand. This is like a product testing phase which may help you come up with a more profitable and attractive range of products for the market.

- **Add diversity to your products:** Do not concentrate your products all into one price range. Be diverse and versatile. Add a number of prices and variety in your product offering. You should be able to cater to a variety of customers. From high-end to low budget potential buyers, all should be targeted.

- **Be flexible while selling:** In the first attempt to sell or during the product testing phase, you need to maintain flexibility in your pricing. Be aware of the buyer's behavior and reaction towards various price ranges. The objective of this initial selling practice is to gain valuable information about the market and customers and not about making a profit. So, remain open to criticism and suggestions.

- **Be open to criticism and respond actively to market signals:** If one or more of your products do not attract a buyer and is not in demand, it is wise to drop it off your list.

These are some of the key considerations that you should keep in mind while making an effort towards turning your woodworking hobby into a full-fledged money-making activity. It is not an overnight project. You need to remain patient and determined. Hard work and devotion towards your goals and objectives is the key to success in any business activity, including wood turning.

Bestselling Woodturning Projects

Product selection is critical:

One of the key factors that can lead to success or failure of the wood turning business is the objects that you select for selling. Like any other business, the product line or marketing offers of the wood turner can make or break the venture.

Product demand is essential for success:

With so many options, you need to come up with products that are easy to produce and easy to sell. Make products that are in demand by the customers. You do not want your creations to keep piling up in storage without anyone being interested in buying them. That's a waste of money, time and effort.

Take ideas from various sources:

For the best options, you need to identify the existing bestselling objects in the market. Once you start your business and are successful in marketing and selling something new that will give rise to your own bestselling products.

Some ideas can be taken for existing wood turners in the industry while online websites and wood craft portals can also become a good source of product identification. You can join social media networks and communities of woodcrafts and woodworkers and get the latest updates and insights on regular basis. Being part of groups and message boards, you are able to share information and get expert advice from other wood turners in the industry. Sharing their personal experiences, they can guide you about the bestselling wood turning products in the market.

Factors underlying the product selection:

Wood turning is a vast field with a large variety of items that you can make and sell. The type of products you can offer in the market depends on the following factors:

- The level of expertise that you have. A wood turner with advanced skills will be able to create more products than one with beginner-level skills.

- The workshop you have also determines your ability to create new and innovative products. Specialized tools for wood turning helps add more detail to the products, making them more attractive and appealing to the customers.

- The storage and display facilities will determine the quantity and size of products that you can make in a given time period. With less storage, your capacity to create and store will decrease.

- The investment that you put into your business, especially in raw materials, will be a big determining factor of the products you select for making and selling. It will also affect all other factors of production.

- The time you put into the production and marketing process will affect your selling capabilities in the market. Simple and small products take less time and are easier to sell without as much effort as large and complex products which require special marketing efforts to sell.

- The creativity and artistry of the wood turner is another factor that can differentiate his products from other players in the market. Unique products are always more likely to become best sellers than those more commonly being sold over a long period of time. Creating wood turning products with your own creativity and artistic touch can make a big difference.

The options found in the wood turning industry are immense. From fruit bowls, salad containers, vases, flower pots to candles stands, and baseball bats, the list of products that can be made with a wood lathe is infinite. Buying a wood lathe for your workshop and mastering this skill allows you to produce hundreds of different products and make lots of money.

Current Categories of Wood Turning Projects:

The wood turning products that are currently selling in the markets are categorized into two different classes.

- The first category is the finished products. These are the wood turning projects that have been completed to the last step of finishing and polishing. They are ready to be used by the customers the moment they are sold.

- The second category of wood turning products sold in the market is semi-finished projects. These are mostly sold as wood turning craft supplies. They include small parts or attachments that are bought and used by other woodworkers for their projects. This is also a very large market and includes thousands of different products of various types.

In most cases the finished products of the wood turner are mostly sold directly to the customers. These include items being sold at the showrooms, display centers, craft shows and flea markets. The semi-finished products are mostly sold through third-party market suppliers. These products are sold in bulk quantities and require large production capacities to meet orders timely.

Another way to make the selling process wide spread across a number of geographic locations is by placing your products with different retailers. You can differentiate your products into categories of gifts, decoration, kitchen accessories, office supplies and wood turning craft supplies. Offering a small commission or flat fee for stocking and selling your products can attract a larger number of vendors and allow you to reach out to a larger customer base.

Bestselling Wood Turning Products in the Market:

Having being used for many, many years, the wood lathe is a miraculous piece of equipment that can help transform a block of wood into a number of useful and beautiful objects. What may seem to be a complex and challenging process for a beginner is quite simple and few hours or even few minutes' work for a professional.

A number of easy do-it-yourself kits and plans can be bought to make things simpler in the beginning. With little practical experience, you won't really need a lot of patterns and plans.

Let us now look at some bestselling wood turning projects which are currently available.

Simple wooden bowls:

This is the most basic and simple item that most wood turners can make in a few minutes on a lathe. Initially, the craftsman will start with a basic solid block of wood in a square or rectangle shape. In the words of woodworkers or turners, it is also known as a 'wooden bowl blank.'

It's a very useful piece of kitchenware that can be utilized for various purposes. From salads to fruits, it can hold a number of different items. Used on coffee tables and in drawing rooms, it adds to the wooden aesthetics of the place. Hence, although it's a very simple product, it's also practical and beautiful.

A dried fruit dish:

Ideal for the cold winter season, you can make small portions or partitions that divide different types of dried fruits in one large dish. It can be cut in several shapes to enhance the beauty and attractiveness of the product. Apart from dried fruits, it can also be used for holding small knickknacks found around the house.

Wooden candle holders:

With a rectangle or circular shape, this product consists of two or more holes that can either hold candles directly in them or candle containers. Either way, it is a great addition to your mantelpiece or on a table or sideboard. Practical, as well as beautiful, this product is small in size and does not require a lot of time and effort.

Handles or knobs for kitchen utensils:

One of the most demanded and widely used form of wood turning in the market is the handle or knob. Small in size, less costly and requiring very little effort, these products are mostly sold in bulk. With its insulation properties, wood is considered a great material for handles and knobs on kitchen utensils and their lids. You can make them in different sizes and shapes, depending on the orders placed with you. It is better to work with specific commercial customers for this kind of product as selling them in retail stores and craft shows is not a very lucrative.

Serving trays:

Wooden serving trays have been used in kitchens for centuries. Even today, they are considered trendy and elegant. Easy to make and less complicated to shape, you can make the tray circular, square or rectangle, whatever appeals to you more. They are less costly and an essential part of every household. People like to buy items whenever they can see it as a good bargain. And if beautifully made, the chances of being bought increases manifold.

Clocks:

Moving out of the kitchen, a very common and widely-used household item is the clock. Wooden clocks have been enjoyed by people for a very long time. They are durable and their design remains evergreen for years and years. Using a lathe, you can make some of the best circular clocks with any type of a wood. However, you need to purchase the rest of the clock parts from a clockmaker. Learn to install these parts yourself or hire the help of a professional. In either case, incorporate all the costs of the production process in order to arrive at a final price. You can place these clocks in various shops, such as furniture stores, gift stores and wood- crafts shops. They are great gifts for weddings, birthdays, anniversaries and many other happy occasions. From the day the clock was invented to the present day, its importance, usefulness and necessity has not diminished. Its demand will remain well into the future.

Decorative items for any room:

Wood is an evergreen material that has been used for decorative purposes for centuries. Various periods of human history have seen the diverse uses of wood in the making of useful objects, as well as decorative items. Its natural ability to make things beautiful has helped woodworkers do wonders. Different types of decorative products like vases, flower pots, containers for marbles or dried flowers and much more can be created using a wood lathe. The choices in this category are immense and infinite. You can copy products made in other materials and convert them into woodworks. Use your creativity and artistic skills to make items that will appeal to people and provide a unique decorative ambiance to their homes and offices. Such products can be easily sold in stores, gift shops, souvenir shops and your own display center or workshop.

Wooden office utilities:

The wood lathe can be used for making small items that can come in handy for a variety of purposes. With its symmetrical workings, the production of small cups, bowls and vases is quite easy and simple. You can make pen holders, paper weights, wire collectors, paper clip containers and a number of other office related items that are useful on any professional's desk. The sky is the limit. You can produce a number of products and add variety and elegance to them with your own ideas and skills. The more neatly and beautifully the object is turned, the more attractive it will become for the potential buyers.

Wooden rolling pins:

Used for bread-making and baking all around the world, the rolling pin is a must have for almost all households. Universally, this versatile kitchen utensil is made from various types of woods. For an expert wood turner making a rolling pin with its circular base or surface is not a complicated process. In fact, it is quite easy and requires less effort. It is a good option for selling to various retail stores. However, you cannot add much creativity and uniqueness to this product. The basic function and usage for all rolling pins remains the same. Hence the competition between producers is quite tough.

Made from one cylindrical piece in the middle, the handles also made from wood can be glued together to complete one of the most useful item in the kitchen.

Chop sticks, spoons and servers:

Adding a little oriental touch to your wood turning projects, chop sticks is one of the easiest options from the East. It requires very little time to make and even less amount of wood as a raw material. They are used for consuming various types of cuisines and are also good for mixing in salads and tossing various food items. Not very widely available, they can be an attractive object to create and sell in the markets. Similar useful objects like wooden spoons and wooden stirring paddles can be also be made using less wood and less effort. They are compulsory items in the kitchen and everyone wants to have at least one or two. So, the market for such products is endless.

Pens:

The last on our list of wood turning objects and at the top of the market's best sellers' list, is the wooden pen which is most attractive for all kinds of customers. Made from small amounts of raw materials, this amazing object can be sold in a variety of designs and sizes. You can diversify your own ideas and bring in the best design that you can make.

These were only a few ideas of some of the bestselling objects in the wood turning industry. The list is infinite and can go on for pages. It is up to the wood turner to generate new and innovative ideas for attractive products that are not just beautiful but also attractive for the consumer.

If you are new at wood turning or looking for ideas and suggestions of what to make and sell, there are a number of sources you can search. The Internet is a vast sea of information with lots of plans, patterns, designs and ideas of objects that can be made and sold using the wood lathe. For example, if you are looking to make a wooden bottle stopper, there could be 20 different patterns and plans that you can follow. With design variations and modification, each product can be given your own unique touch.

You do not only find plans and diagrams, but also step-by-step instructions on its production, the tools used for the process, detailed descriptions in terms of size and make, and finished pictures of the projects.

Although the list of the bestselling wood turning products that you can make and sell is huge, some common items are listed below for your consideration:

1.   Alabaster
2.   Baby Rattles
3.   Balls
4.   Balusters
5.   Bells
6.   Bird Feeders
7.   Baseball Bats
8.   Bottle stoppers
9.   Bowls
10.   Birdhouses
11.   Boxes
12.   Brushes
13.   Bracelets

14.   Cake Stands

15.   Captive Rings

16.   Chinese Balls

17.   Chessboards and Pieces

18.   Coffee Cups

19.   Coffee Grinders

20.   Decorative Boxes and Bowls

21.   Yo-Yo's

22.   Table Legs

23.   Stands

24.   Stools

25.   Stamp Holders

26.   Wig Stands

27.   Vases

28.   Toys

29.   Trivets

30.   Tops

31.   Tool Handles

32.   Tea-light holders

33.   Urns

34.   Toothpick Holders

35.   Walking sticks

This is just a list of some of the items that can be made by using a wood lathe or wood turning skills. The options are infinite and the sky is the limit. Creativity and utility are the key to success for creating a bestseller in the market.

Best Selling Wood Crafts to Make and Sell

In the previous section, the bestselling objects to make and sell from wood turning has been described. However, wood crafting is much bigger and more diversified. Using varied skills and crafts, you can make some unique and different types of objects from this natural material.

Woodcraft is ancient:

Wood has been used as a medium for making things for human needs and requirements since ancient times. Studies and historical research reveals that all civilizations from the past until today have used wood as one of their prime sources of raw materials. Historical evidence shows that wood has been used in the past for several important purposes some of which are listed below:

- Housing and shelters
- Weapons and defensive tools
- Craft tools
- Kitchen and cooking utensils
- Decorative ornamentation
- Personal usage items, like walking sticks
- Toys
- Landmarks
- Furniture for human needs
- And much more.

The list of the objects that can be made from wood is large and wide. It all depends on the availability of raw materials and the skills of the craftsman.

Making wooden objects for profit:

1. What to make?

For anyone who is starting his or her new business venture using wood crafts, the first question that might come to mind is what to make and how to sell it to make profit. This is not a very easy question. Like all other business ventures, doing a bit of market research can help you come up with some great answers. But being a skill-based craft, you also need to assess your own capabilities, capacity and passion of making those things.

2. Skill and demand:

Match your skills and production capacity with the products that are high in demand in the market and can be sold to make significant profit.

3. Gather information:

Apart from asking family members, friends and coworkers, you can also do some primary market research with retailers and stores. The internet is also a good option to find all kinds of information. From new business venture ideas to exact product descriptions and plans can be found in this virtual database. This is a big advantage that people have today that was not available in the past.

Some Product Categories to Work On:

Some great options for you to start your woodcraft business may include the following categories:

Children's toys:

Not very long ago, wooden toys were popular in many parts of the world. Having toys made from wood was not an unsual thing. But now things are very different. With so much development in the toy industry, finding toys that are wooden and made by hand is considered a novelty. Wooden toys are considered collectors' items where the sellers are allowed to charge premuim price for such products. Being more expensive than regular toys, these products have a smaller market when it comes to customers. However, the niche for wooden toys is still prevalent and people are willing to pay high prices for their love of them.

For this reason, the woodwork markets rate toys made from wood as bestselling items. Made with superior quality wood, these toys are more durable and safes than regular plastic toys. There are many parents who want their kids to play with these special toys for safety reasons.

Keeping in mind the sensitive nature of children and their parents, woodworkers should pay extra attention while making these toys.

You should be careful to avoid using any unsafe materials and designs.

Some characteristics that you should ensure when making wooden toys are:

- Safety of the children
- Durability and long-lasting usage
- Sturdiness and stability
- High quality materials
- Best craftsmanship.

Baby cradles and cribs:

This product category is a permanent niche in the market. As long as there are babies in the world, the need for cradles and cribs will continue to exist. With slight modifications and variations, the basic structure of the crib and cradle remains the same.

It is a very important piece of furniture that is needed by every parent. With so much love and tenderness in the child-parent relationship, every parent wants their kid to have the best. These days, most people want custom-designed furniture for their children in their nurseries. With so much awareness in the media and on the Internet, new designs and innovations can be found for these wooden furniture pieces. Woodworking in the children's category does not remain limited to cribs and cradles only. There are other pieces of furniture, such as

- Tables
- Chairs
- Storage cupboards
- Beds
- And an assortment of other objects

Cribs, however, are much more popular in woodcraft and their demand is quite big. Like wooden toys, parents are very concerned about the quality of the product and its safety. Paying extra to using superior quality materials and the best craftsmanship is a common practice in this product category.

Bookcases:

What could be more entertaining for a hobbyist or woodworker than a book? Books of one kind or another are always present in every home and office. So, everyone needs to have a book shelf or bookcase somewhere in their home or office. The demand for this product never fades out. Although the designs may vary according to current trends and home fashion, the overall use and function of the product remains the same.

Keeping in mind the latest trends and requirements, design something that is modern yet compact. Add your own creativity to the product and make it unique for multipurpose usage. Your product should not just be useful but it should also have a good physical appearance and be pleasant to look at.

Picture frames:

If you had to walk around a hundred houses, every one of them would have picture frames in one form or another. Today, picture frames are made from different materials and in different ways. But the classic wooden picture frame remains a top choice for most people. With its versatility and artistic appearance, it is a simple yet high demand product. Using a little artistic touch, each woodworker can create his or her own master piece which will stand out among others for its uniqueness. This product remains a top seller in the woodworking industry with continuous demand in the market. The designs may vary but the basic manufacturing and structure of all wooden picture frames remains similar.

Boxes:

Big boxes, small boxes, jewelry boxes, toy boxes, tool boxes, nut boxes and many other types of boxes are found in every household.

Made from different materials, they are of immense use in terms of storage and function. Wood is a great material to make all kinds of boxes.

Most woodworkers find it easy and simple to make a box. They can be made of high quality materials and this enhances the durability of these storage facilitators. Keep your options open and use your artistic talent to generate new ideas for boxes. Create boxes of variable sizes to attract a larger number of potential customers.

Birdhouses:

The outdoors provides ample opportunities and ideas for woodworkers. From popular gardening objects to tool shed items to general decorative items. There are a large number of outdoor projects that you can make and sell to your customers. We all want our houses and offices to look good and wood gives a real rustic and natural style to the ambiance.

Bird houses of various designs and styles are popular wooden objects used in big and small gardens and even in apartments with small balconies. Those who already have pet birds will be willing to pay much more for good designs.

The bird lovers around the world want to observe and look at birds chirping in their surroundings. Adding a lively feeling to the entire place, the birds feel comfortable with bird feeders and water containers placed alongside their homely wooden structures. Bird houses are one of the bestselling wooden products in the market today.

Blanket chests:

A bit large in size, this product is undoubtedly a very useful piece of furniture around the house. With its large storage capacity, it can be used for multiple purposes. Designed for bedrooms to store blankets, cushions and pillows, this product cannot be made better in any other material. Wood is the perfect blanket chest material as it is durable and looks good as well.

In every household, there are several small and big items that need to be carefully stored away. Keeping them safe in a blanket chest is a great idea to avoid clutter in the room. In order for your product to be successful in the market and to stand out among similar competitors, you need to focus on quality, simplicity, finish and durability.

Wooden spoons and ladles:

These are kitchen and cooking related objects, the demand for which has never dropped. With little variation in design, these products are mostly bought impulsively without too much thought.

Woodworkers can produce them in various designs and sizes to attract a larger customer base. Although materials like plastic and metal have taken a large chunk out of the market for this product, wooden cooking utensils are still the most used and liked by traditional chefs.

Technically, you can make most wood projects with hand tools. But some just go faster than others.

Name plates and planters:

Many people like to install name plates outside their apartments and homes. The wooden plates add some natural style to these decorative yet useful objects. They can be modified for attractiveness and some space can be added to place a small plant. This makes it more beautiful so that it stands out with the addition of the plant. You can also add flowers to this planter. It can be placed on a pillar, gate or main door.

Small wooden tables:

Tables are very useful around the house and office. They can be utilized for various functions and purposes. There are a number of different types and sizes. Wood is the most commonly used material for making tables worldwide. A good wood craftsman will combine functionality with physical beauty to make the table a best seller.

Using simple hand tools and equipment, small tables used for corners and room sidings is a great way to earn some good money. A table is an essential piece of furniture that is used invariably by most people all over the world.

Wooden stools:

Just like a wooden table, a stool is a great furniture piece used for sitting and resting purposes. Alternatively, to a comfortable chair, stools can be used in various parts of house and office, as well as for outdoor activities and purposes. It can be used in the garden, in a children's play area, in workshops, and even for picnics and days out on the beach. Woodworkers should ensure that they are made from good quality wood that is light to carry but which also provides the right amount of sturdiness and strength to withstand the weight of the user.

Stools can be modified in design and size to meet the specific needs of the buyer. You can also take orders for children rooms and nurseries.

Wine stands and racks:

Have you ever been in a wine cellar? The only thing that you can find in abundance other than wine bottles are racks and shelves to hold those bottles. Alternatively, these racks can also be made with metal, but metallic racks are prone to rust and can wear out over time. Wood is a much durable and traditional material used worldwide for making wine racks.

A good wood worker should be able to make such racks with ease and not too much effort. You can offer various sizes to accommodate the space available in homes, basements or attics. An ideal stand should be able to hold the regular-sized bottles with ease for placement and removal. Keep the measurements accurate and precise to avoid any mishaps.

Wooden arm chairs:

Suitable for more advanced and professional woodworkers, you can find a number of different designs and plans on the Internet for comfortable armchairs. With both traditional and modern designs in fashion, people use them in various locations in the house. Whether they are buying it for the study, sunroom, garden or living room, an ideal arm chair should be able to provide the comfort and convenience to ease out the tiredness of the entire day. Offering folding capabilities, the woodworker can enhance the appeal of his or her product and increase its demand in the market for the storage and space sensitive people.

Paper weights:

Paper weights made from various heavy materials are used in offices, educational institutions and even at home in study rooms and libraries. Wood can be made into a good paper weight as well. It is a simple yet affordable product that can be made in various attractive designs but at a low cost. Because paper weights are placed on important papers and documents, woodworkers should ensure that the wood used is dry and does not produce any types of stains or patches.

Wooden tablet stands:

With so much technology in our hands, we often want to give them some rest. For those who are technology savvy yet a bit traditional in their likings, a wooden tablet stand is what they might need. Made from a simple wooden block, the object is a woodworker's wonder. It does not have any joints or glue usage in its making.

With so many mobile and tablet users worldwide, the product is a great way to make some money through your woodworking skills. All iPad and tablet users are sure to give some serious thought to buying this beautiful and handy piece of art.

Drawer organizers:

Sometimes making a product popular depends upon how well you create a niche for it. The way it is marketed and promoted to the customer can make a big difference. The wooden drawer organizer is one such product that can draw a lot of attention if it is marketed in the right way. If you are selling it online, then market it by sharing pictures and videos of how useful it can be. Similarly, if selling it at a store or display center, properly display its utility with a drawer to highlight its usefulness.

Drawer organizers are a very simple and easy project for woodworkers. And it is on the list of best selling items of wood because of its immense usefulness and benefits. You can also make it your best seller by improvising the designs and bringing in more innovations to this old but useful product.

Office trays:

If you want to keep your office or study desk organized, having a tray for all your loose items and files is a great idea. Wooden trays are popular because of their aesthetic quality and durability. Trays of different sizes and designs can be used for different purposes. Files can be organized in larger trays while paper pins, erasers and sharpeners can be stored in smaller trays.

Wall shelves and racks:

Contemporary, yet functional and useful, shelves can add a lot to those empty walls. They can be made in a variety of designs, shapes, sizes and styles. These are the kind of things that are signature best sellers of wood material. No other material can become a good alternative for them. Whether the customer wants to use them for books, crockery or other items, the choices are unlimited.

Wooden pots and planters:

When talking about gardens and lawns, what more can you want than a beautiful wooden planter in your natural habitat? Ideally, such wooden pots and planters can also be used in drawing rooms, living rooms and other indoor spaces. When it comes to design and pattern, you can do various experiments. You can also offer customized pots for special themes and home décor.

Combining woodcraft with a little bit of metal work can also add to the attractiveness of this product.

Final Thoughts about Transforming Your Wood Crafting Ideas and Turning a Hobby into a Money-Making Activity:

Wood is a naturally occurring material that is available in abundance. It has been used by people since time immemorial. From historical civilizations to the present day, it is one of the most common and widely used production materials on the planet. From offices, houses, kitchens, restaurants, factories, cafes, educational institutions, hospitals to anywhere else where people work and live, wooden objects can be found.

Used to make essential items like furniture, doors, windows, floorings, roofs and even walls, wooden houses are a real master piece for any craftsman in this field. People who are interested and passionate about this material, like to work with it with a specific set of skills. They either learn these skills from professionals or they develop them through personal experimentation.

Woodworking or wood turning is a hobby for a large number of people. They love to make wooden objects for themselves and for the benefit of others. They mostly do this activity in their free time and do not charge a dime for it. In fact, most hobbyists like to spend their money on making their hobby more interesting and fun. They take money from their own pockets to buy raw materials, supplies and tools and give the final products to other people without accepting any money in exchange. It gives them pleasure, as well as motivating them through the appreciation and recognition of their efforts.

However there in no harm is turning your hobby into a profession. It means earning from an activity that you love to do. Something that you are passionate about and at the same time can make you money while you practice your passion. This is an ideal situation which not many people get to achieve in their lives. So, whether you are doing it as a full-time livelihood or as a part-time hobby for some extra money, there are some essential guidelines and tips that you need to keep in mind for your woodcraft venture to be successful.

Here are some basic recommendations and guidelines:

1. Attitude is everything:

Mold your goals and objectives around your passion. Make wood crafting objects and sell them to customers as fast as you can. Bring in the 'make and sell' attitude and let it flourish through this process. Your skills and craftsmanship is the underlying factor for running this business. They are free and you can improve them over time. So, being the best and considering yourself the best is necessary for others to recognize what you make and sell.

2. Quality is everything:

When it comes to the woodworker, attitude is everything. When it comes to the woodworking objects, quality is everything. Ensuring the high quality of raw materials and high quality craftsmanship is necessary for the success of your wood crafting business. With such a large market and so much information flow on the Internet, the making of popular wood objects is quite easy. The concept of competition is also left behind if you are producing the same things.

The only factor that you will make you stand out from your rival players is the quality of your products and the superiority of the finish. This does not mean that you can come up with the best in just one night. Practice and make improvements over time. Give special attention to dimensions and measurements and ensure accuracy and precision in every piece.

3. Be optimistic:

If you are also looking to turn your hobby into some extra cash, be optimist and confident. Having an attitude of moving forward and taking the right initiative is what you need. Working on your passion and also making money from it is like a dream come true. Do not let it slip it away.

4. It won't happen overnight:

Turing your woodworking hobby into a business is not a one-day job. It's a lengthy process that may take some time to develop and mature. Although, these days you get a lot of help from online sources and platforms for both making and selling wooden items, it's not as simple as you think.

You need to remain patient and avoid hasty decisions and actions. No business can run without time and effort. You can make the business run smoothly but with a gradual pace.

5. Maintain good supplier relations:

Like all other types of manufacturing businesses, having reliable suppliers of raw materials and other supplies is vital for the success of your business. You should be able to rely on the supplier for urgent deliveries and affordable rates. Quality is the key to products in the wood crafting business. The better-quality wood you use, the better the final products. Therefore, it is very important that you select a supplier that has a good reputation and who can supply the best wood at the best price.

6. Pricing is critical:

The four Ps of marketing are applicable to the woodworking business as well. With due importance given to product, place and promotion, price plays a vital role in the buying decision of the customer. With too high a price for a simple utility object, the customers will be put off for good. With too low a price, people might perceive that the products are of a low quality.

So, you need to price the product after a detailed expense break down and with the ability to recover all the costs that has been spent in the making of the item. With carefully calculated profit margins, you will be able to gain a lot of new customers and make money through your wood crafting.

Best of Luck!

There you have it, a detailed insight on how you can transform wood crafting or wood turning skills into a profession together with the important factors that you need to keep in mind for its ultimate success. Follow these guidelines and select bestseller products for your business. Determination, hard work and confidence in your ability will ensure you move ahead in a fast and positive direction in the woodworking industry.

Check out some of the other JD-Biz Publishing books

Gardening Series on Amazon

Download Free Books!

http://MendonCottageBooks.com

Country Life Books

Amazing Animal Book Series

Learn To Draw Series

How to Build and Plan Books

Entrepreneur Book Series

Our books are available at

1. Amazon.com

2. Barnes and Noble

3. Itunes

4. Kobo

5. Smashwords

6. Google Play Books

Download Free Books!

http://MendonCottageBooks.com

Publisher

JD-Biz Corp

P O Box 374

Mendon, Utah 84325

http://www.jd-biz.com/

Printed in Great Britain
by Amazon

41493286R00046